NEV
UP(

DIALECT

A Selection of Words and Anecdotes
from Around Newcastle upon Tyne

By

Kate Sanderson

BRADWELL
BOOKS

Published by Bradwell Books
9 Orgreave Close Sheffield S13 9NP
Email: books@bradwellbooks.co.uk

British Library Cataloguing in Publication Data: a catalogue
record for this book is available from the British Library.

1st Edition
ISBN: 9781902674506
Print: Gomer Press, Llandysul, Ceredigion SA44 4JL
Design by: JenksDesign

Photograph Credits
Photographs of the Hoppings, Harold Hill and Son Ltd., 1950s interior
Kenton, Sage, Baltic, Millennium Bridge © John Sanderson
Photographs of Central Arcade and Penny Bazaar
© Catherine Sanderson
Photograph of the Mark Toney ice cream van © Mark Toney & Co. Ltd.
All other photographs © Newcastle Libraries.

INTRODUCTION

We were standing on the platform in Nuremberg Railway Station in September 2012, with heavy showers battering on the roof, when we struck up a conversation with another couple from the North East and fell into a discussion of how many words in the Newcastle upon Tyne area dialect sound very similar to the same words in German. Travelling by train onwards to Brussels and then by Eurostar to London, similarities to Scandinavian languages were noted, such as the Danish and Norwegian words for home being hjem, spelled differently but with the same pronunciation as the Newcastle dialect word hyem. Brian Johnson and my husband John, both born and brought up in the city, considered the changes in dialect from when they were lads and from when Harold Hill and Son Ltd., founded by John's grandfather, published *A Northumberland and Durham Word Book – The Living Dialect* by Cecil Geeson in 1969. On returning from his trip, Brian was laid up in bed for a while and started listing dialect words he thought were still in use, a pastime which led to the beginnings of this book.

In times past, Newcastle's quayside was full of international hustle and bustle as it traded with many parts of the world, exporting coal, cement, chemicals and machinery and importing grain, meat, fruit and butter along with many other goods. The old Baltic flour mill, still standing proud on the Gateshead quayside, is a testament to this and it is still in use today as a contemporary art space. The Tyne saw seamen and workers from the Netherlands, Germany and Scandinavia as well as ship's crews from London's East End, Liverpool and Glasgow. Coal on its way abroad often went through Amsterdam in the late eighteenth century, and herring fishing also encouraged workers from different countries to visit the North East as they followed the route of the herring. Quite a few of the bonny keelmen who loaded the coal from the staithes on the Tyne onto the collier ships were Scottish, and this may be why some words used in Newcastle are also familiar in my native Glasgow.

It is quite difficult these days to say exactly where this dialect begins and ends because of the movement of people, the influence of television programmes set in the North East and the tradition of passing words and phrases, as well as songs and stories, from one generation to the next. The last remaining pit at Ellington closed in 2005, so Pitmatic, the dialect of the coal miners, can no longer be used in its original setting. However, many of the words have come into general usage and are included here, as well as others that may be useful if reading old poems and books.

Why has Geordie not been mentioned? The dialect spoken in Tyneside was called Geordie by Scott Dobson in 1969, in his very humorous book, *Larn Yersel' Geordie*. However, this leads to the very controversial subject of who can rightly call themselves a Geordie. Everyone has their own opinion and reckons they are right, whether their decision is based on being born within sight of the tidal section of the River Tyne, being born in Newcastle, being a follower of King George, or perhaps it is after George Stephenson, or even St George on the back of gold coins!

Collecting reminiscences of Newcastle has been a rewarding experience with interesting conversations, detailed discussions and, of course, generous hospitality. Brian Johnson believes that the Newcastle dialect varies, even within the city. *"The location is important. I recall a song in a pantomime at either the Royal or the Empire, to the tune of 'If you ever go across the sea to Ireland': 'If you ever go across the bridge to Byker, it's a very lovely place to which to go. And the folk who live across the bridge in Byker, speak a language that the Jesmond folk don't know'. And Benwell folk might have struggled a bit there as well!"*

Kate Sanderson

A

Aa – I

Aad – I did

Aa wis palatic an aa fell doon – I was very drunk and I fell over

Aal – all

Aal together like the folks iv Sheels – All together like the folks of Shields. This is a phrase from a Tyneside song of the early 1800s which has come to mean a close huddle of family and friends

Aalreet, aareet – alright, can be used instead of hello

Aa've a mind tiv – I think I might

Aboon – above

Aboot – about

Ackers – loose change

Afear'd – afraid

Again – against

Afta – after

Agyen – again

Ah – I

Ah'll – I will

Ain – own

Alang – along

A'm gannin' – I'm going

An' all – as well

An' such as – and so on, etc…

A

A one – one

Aud – old

Aught – anything

Auld – old

Aw – I

Aye – yes

B

Babby – baby

Back end – autumn

Back ower – return

Bagie, baggie – turnip with white flesh, a Swedish turnip, swede

Bairn – child

Bait – food taken to work, packed lunch

Bank – hill, as in Byker Banks

Bank – above ground at a pit

Banksman – man in control at the top of the pit shaft

Barley – to reserve, to bag - mostly used by children

Beck – stream

Bed-happins – bedclothes

Beor – beer

Beeskep – beehive made of straw

Bide – wait

B

Bigg – barley

Bizzem – a term of abuse applied to a female. 'She's a reet bizzem'

Blabb – to talk out of turn

Blabbermouth – someone who can't keep a secret

Black Bullets – a mint-flavoured hard-boiled sweet

Blackclock – cockroach

Blaked – yellowish, pale, to get drunk

Blather – to talk nonsense

Bleech – a gale with snow or rain

Blob – overtime. 'Are ye blobbin' the neet?'

Bogie – a box mounted on wheels used by children

Bogie – truck used on the quayside by cartmen

Boggle – ghost

Boilie – bread with warm milk and sugar

Bonny lass – a pretty girl

Bonny lad – friend, mate, sometimes used as a greeting. 'Hay way there, bonny lad'

Bool – to bowl, such as 'to bool a hoop'

Brahma – excellent

Brass – money

Bray – to beat, to knock on a door

Breeks – trousers

Broon – brown

Broons – bottles of Newcastle Brown Ale

B

Bubble – weep

Buff – bare skin

Bullets – sweets

Bumler bee – bumblebee

Burn – small stream

Buzzer – the steam whistle that announced starting and finishing times at the pit

C

Cack-handed – left-handed, clumsy

Cakhouse – outside toilet

Caad – cold

Caidie – a flat cap

Cannie – candle

Canny – alright

Canny good – more than alright

Canny lad – a nice boy

Canny – good and reliable person. 'She's canny'

Contraband – cigarettes, matches, lighter, all items not allowed down the pits

Carlings – dried peas steeped in water and fried in butter

Carling Sunday – fifth Sunday in Lent when carlings were served

Champion – first class

C

Chare – a narrow lane in the town

Charver – clubber or rough person

Choppy – pony feed

Claes – clothes

Claggum – glue, sticky toffee

Claggy – sticky

Clamming for a drink – very thirsty

Clarts – wet sticky mud

Clarty – muddy, mucky

Cleg – horsefly

Clemmed – hungry, thirsty

Click – to pull threads in clothing

Click – to meet someone you get on well with. 'We just clicked'

Clickin' – excellent

Clip – hit. 'A clip roond the ear'

Clootie – cloth. Clootie pudding is a pudding steamed in a cloth

Clod – a stupid person

Codger – an old person with old fashioned views. 'Dina pay onae attention tae him, he's jist an old codger'

Cogly – unsteady

Coin – turn, turn around, spin

Coo – cow

Copple the creels – turn a somersault

Corby – raven

The Central Arcade with its glass barrelled roof, tiles in shades of yellow and brown, and galleries with iron railings is more often called Window's Arcade as their Music Shop has been there since 1908

C

Cotterels – loose change

Cowp – overturn, tip out

Cowp your creels – turn a somersault

Crack – good conversation, chat, news, banter

Cracket – small three-legged stool

Crake – wooden rattle

Cree – shed

Crib – bed

Croggie – a ride on the crossbars of a bicycle

Crowdy – type of porridge made with oatmeal, water and milk, sometimes with butter, dripping or treacle added

C

Cuddy – donkey, small horse

Cuddy-duck – an eider-duck, a favourite of St Cuthbert

Cundy – sewer

Cush – excellent, cool

Cushat – wood pigeon, dove

Cushty – excellent, cool

Cushy – cow, easy. A cushy number is an easy job

Cutty – a short pipe for tobacco

Cut – a narrow passage between houses, a lane

D

Daffy – smarten up

Daggy – drizzly rain

Darking – eavesdropping

Dayleet – daylight

Dee – die

Deed – dead

Deed bad – very poorly

Deil – devil

Dene – deep valley

Deppity's kist – box for keeping tools, papers, first aid equipment

Dhan-end – a buoy at the end of a line of lobster pots

D

Dickies – head lice, nits

Dinaa – don't

Div – do

Divvin't – do not

Doll – to hit

Dolly-muck – small pieces of coal

Dolly-wash – coal dust

Doon – down, dejected

Doon-bye – down there

Dottle – a bit left over

Dooshy – good

Dorty – dirty

Dreich – referring to weather – gloomy, wet

Drouthy – thirsty

Dyke – wall, hedge

Dry-dyke – dry-stone wall

Duckat – pigeon loft

Duds – clothes

Dunch – bump, crash into, knock against

Dut – bowler hat, or nowadays a woolly hat

D'ye – do you

Dyell – wood

E

Eggtaggle – a waste of time
Endlang – lengthways

F

Fadge – round loaf of bread
Fair up – referring to weather - will improve
Fall in wi – meet up with
Fash – trouble, bother
Fast – immovable
Femmer – weak, frail or slender
Fettle – good condition. To fettle something is to fix it
Fine fettle – good health
Fladge – snowflake
Flanged – drunk
Fleet – net used for trawling herring
Flit – move house
Flithers – limpets
Flittermouse – bat
Fogs – first
Foisty – damp, musty, mouldy
Forkytail – earwig
Forst – first
Foy – pilot boat

Entrance to the Central Arcade

F

Fratch – quarrel
Frae – from
Frumenty – porridge with sugar and spices
Fullikin – cheating at marbles
Funning – joking
Fyece – face

G

Gadgie – old man
Gaffer – boss
Galloway – pony, pit pony

G

Galluses – braces for trousers

Gan – go

Gan canny – take care, goodbye

Gannin' hyem – going home

Gansey – woolly jumper

Gat – got

Garth – yard

Gaup – to stare. 'What are ye gauping at?'

Gawn – going

Gawn – pull funny faces

Geordie – a colliery safety lamp invented by George Stephenson

Get wrang off – to be told off by

Gimmer – young ewe

Ginny-longlegs – cranefly

Gisa gan – give me a turn

Give ower, man! – that's enough!

Give ye what for – to give you a telling off

Glass alley – a glass marble of good quality

Glead – bird of prey

Goller – holler

Gowdspink – goldfinch

Gowk – apple core

Grand – great, fine

Greeting – weeping

H

Haad, haud – hold

Haar – sea fret

Hacky – dirty

Haddaway – go away

Halfers – to share half each. 'Will ye gan halfers wi me?'

Hailers – ropes used to haul keelboats

Hansell – to use for the first time or wear in something new, like shoes

Hanted – become accustomed to

Hap – overcoat, topcoat, shawl

Het – hot

Heed – head

Hey-up – look out

Hinny, hinney – friend, honey, sweetheart

Hitchy-dabber – hop-scotch

Hitty-missy – randomly

Hoo – how

Hoose – house

Hoppin's, Hoppings – a travelling fair that still comes to Newcastle's Town Moor every year

Howay – come on

Howay, the lads! – come on, Newcastle United!

Howlet – owl

How's it gannin', like? – How are you doing?

Hoy – to throw, or a game of pitch 'n' toss

H

Hoyers – loose change
Hoyin' oot time – closing time, especially of pubs
Hoy-oot – throwing coins out of a car at a wedding
Hump – carry
Hunkers – haunches
Hyem – home

I

Inbye – inside the home, also a command to a sheepdog
Impittent – impudent
In the buff – naked
Ivvory – every

J

Jarping – egg rolling at Easter
Jells – originally wooden planks used to cover the hold of a keelboat. Now used more generally to mean pieces of wood
Joon – June
Jowl – to tap
Jowling – tapping on the walls and roofs in the pits to check their condition and decide if they are safe

K

Keek – take a quick look, peek

Keeker, keeka – foreman in the coal mines

Keel, keelboat – the boats that transferred coal from the riverside staithes to the ships

Keelmen, keelers – crew of keelboats

Keggy-eye – a black eye

Keks – trousers

Ken – know or remember

Keps – type of iron chocks that the cage rested on in a pit shaft

Ket – children's sweets such as Dolly Mixtures or Jelly Babies

Kibble – a large tub for rubbish

Kiddar, kidder – a youngster, also a friendly term for a younger person or friend

Kinks – laughter. To be in kinks means to be in fits of laughter

Kist – chest for relics, tools, clothes or treasure

Knaa – know

Knacks – hurts a lot

L

Lace – to beat, wallop

Lad – boy

Ladgeful – bad

Laelock – lilac

Lang – long

Larn – to teach

Lass – girl, young woman, wife

Laverock – skylark

Leazes – pasture land

Like – used at the end of a spoken sentence, usually a question. 'How's that, like?'

Ling – heather

Lonnen – lane

Logger – moth

Lop – a flea. 'As fit as a lop'

Loppy dog – a flea-ridden dog

Louse – let go. 'Louse hold of it'

Low – a light or flame (pronounced to rhyme with cow)

Lug – ear, handle

Lum – chimney

Lush – very good

The 'Naughty-Ninety Girls' at the Hoppings, late 1950s

M

Ma – my

Ma ain – my own

Mam – mum

Maddle – fond of, or confused

Magpies, The – affectionate name for the Newcastle United football team

Mair – more

Maist – most

M

Maistor – master, shopkeeper

Makem – someone who comes from Sunderland

Man – used for both men and woman as an exclamation or a form of address

Marra – friend, workmate

Marra, marrow – to match items like socks, gloves etc

Mask – to infuse tea, brew

Maw – my

Mawk – maggot, miserable person

Mazer – someone who is amazing, eccentric or weird

Mebbies – maybe

Mek – make

Mell – hammer

Merle – blackbird

Me sel' – myself

Midden – rubbish heap. 'This hoose is just like a midden'

Midden-craa – carrion crow

Midgy – small oil lamp

Mind – remember

Mind tiv – thinking about

Mind yon time? – do you remember that time?

Mister – man, shopkeeper

Mint – excellent

Mizzle – fine rain or mist

Monged – muddled, intoxicated

M

Mooth – mouth
Mortal – very drunk
Muckle – very
Muggles – glass marbles
Mullered – drunk
Munter – ugly person
Myed – made

N

Na – no
Naebody – nobody
Naggie – Hallowe'en turnip lantern
Naught – nothing
Ne – no, as in 'ne-where'
Neb – nose
Nebby – nosy
Neet – night
Nettie, netty – outside toilet
Newcassel – Newcastle upon Tyne, with emphasis on 'cas'
Newcastle Broon – Newcastle Brown Ale
Nippy – cold
Nivvor – never

N

Noo – now
Not ower grand – not very well
Notha – another
Nowt – nothing
Nyem – name

O

Ony – any
Onywhere – anywhere
Oor – our, hour
Oot – out
Outbye – outside
Ower – over
Ower-bye – over that way
Owt – anything

P

Paddick – frog
Paid oot – tired, exhausted
Palatic – very drunk
Panacalty – cornbeef hash made in a frying pan

P

Panhaggerty – dish of potatoes, onions, cheese and sometimes leftover meat

Parky – fussy, choosy

Paste eggs – hard-boiled eggs decorated for rolling at Easter

Pease puddin' – made from dried split-peas

Penny loppy – cheap cinema ticket, with the added chance of catching fleas!

Pet – a term of endearment used for both men and women

Pikelet – a type of thin crumpet

Pinge – whinge

Pit – coal mine

Pitman – collier, coal miner

Pitmatic – the dialect of coal miners

Pit-yakker – pitman, coal miner

Play the wag – play truant

Play war with – be very, very angry with someone

Plodge – paddle in the sea

Plother – wet and muddy

Polis – police

Poond – pound

Poor'd – poured

Poss tub – a washing tub shaped like a barrel, where clothes were pounded with a poss-stick

Prog – to poke or prick

P

Proggy mat – a mat made by poking strips of rags through holes in a hessian base
Put yersel' away – get on with the job, work harder

Q

Quicks – young hawthorn trees used for hedging
Quicken-tree – mountain ash tree

R

Radgie-gadgie – angry old man
Rax – to stretch
Reeks – smokes (as in a chimney), or smells strongly (reeks o' broon ale)
Reet – right
Rive – rent, tear, scratch
Rolley – small wagon or lorry
Roond – round
Round the doors – nearby

S

Sackless – not very bright, incompetent

Santy – Santa Claus, Father Christmas

Sark – shirt

Scallion – spring onion

Scran – food

Scrammil – scramble

Scranchings – bits and pieces of hard fried batter that used to come with fish and chips

Scunner – an intense dislike, aversion

Sea-fret – a coastal fog that, at times, also rolls ups up the Tyne

Segs – the half-moon-shaped metal tacks that were put on the heels and toes of shoes and boots to give them longer wear

Set yer on – give you a job

Set away – get going, free, start up

Shabby – not feeling very well

Sharper – quicker

Shot – to throw

Shud – should

Shuggy-boats – swing boats at the Hoppings and other fairgrounds

Shuggy-shew – rope swing

Singin' hinny – cake with currants baked on a griddle

Skelp – slap

S

Skemmy – pigeon

Skep – straw basket

Skinch – a truce

Skinchees – calling a truce in children's games

Smit – an infection, to infect

Smitten – taken a fancy to

Sneck – door latch

Somewhat – something

Spelk – a splinter, or a very thin person

Spennish – liquorice

Snaggin' – cutting tops off turnips

Snanny – turnip with orange flesh

Spuggy – a sparrow or any small bird

Staithe – a landing stage where coal was loaded onto boats

Stanchels – bars, uprights

Stannin' – standing

Starving – very cold

Starvation – extremely cold. 'It's starvation in here'

Stot – bounce

Stotty, stotty-cake – round, flat loaf

Stotty-bun – a large, flat round roll sometimes topped with cheese

Stowed-off – a place that is really full, crowded, packed

Strite – straight

Stuck fast – can't be moved, jammed

Stumer – an outrageous idea, unexpected action or unusual person – either because they are exceptionally stupid or very shrewd

Taa – toe

Tab – cigarette

Tae – to

That 'ill larn ye – that will teach you

Tappy-lappy – in a rush

Tatties, tetties – potatoes

Teem – to pour out, empty

Teeming – pouring with rain

Teeming bye, teeming ower – setting aside coal instead of putting it on the wagons

Teld, telt – told

The day – today

The lads – Newcastle United football team

The morn – the morning

The neet – tonight

The Toon – Newcastle upon Tyne

The Toon Army – Newcastle United supporters

Tiggy – children's game of tag

Tiv – to

T

Toon – town

Toot – to look out, spy on

Tosser – a coin of little value, or a silly person

Trashing – tiring, exhausting

Tret – treated. 'How wis ye tret?'

Trots – a bit of wood with short line and hook attached, used for fishing from the beach

Tyuk – took

Tun wheyte – very heavy

Twisting – moaning, whinging, quarrelling

U

Up-a-height – high up

V

Vast o'folk – lots of people, a crowd

W

Wad – would

War, wor – were

Wark – work

Watter – water

Waup – curlew

Weans – children

Weel – well

Weel oiled – drunk (but not palatic!)

Wes – was

Wham – stomach

What for – why

Wey – why

Wey aye! – certainly, yes, definitely

Wey aye, man – OK, mate

Whinge – whine, complain

Whisht – be quiet

Why – well

Wifie – an old or uneducated woman, whether married or not

Wi, wiv – with

Winna – won't

Wirra – with a

Wis – was

Wivoot – without

Wor – our, were

W

Worabbot – what about?

Wor kid – our brother, or sister

Wor lass – my wife, girlfriend, partner

Worm – dragon, serpent

Wotcheor – hello

Wrang – wrong, or get into trouble, get told off

Wrought out – pit or coal seam where all the coal had been removed

Y

Yakker – worker

Yallow, yalla – yellow

Yammor – whine on, talk incessantly

Yark – strike, thrash, a sharp blow

Ye – you

Ye knaa what ah mean, like? – you understand, don't you?

Yer, yor – your

Yet – still

Yon – that one over there

Yous – plural of you

Countin' the coal wagons

In the pits the horn of a tup (a ram) was sent up with every twentieth wagon of coal so that a tally could be kept of the wagons. The last wagon of coal taken to the surface at the end of each year was decorated with lighted candles, placed on top of the coal by the pit laddies – a tradition that died out in the nineteenth century.

Children in Sandgate outside a grocer's shop with jars of sweets in the window, 1898

Nursery rhymes

The Little Fishy
Come here my little Jackey,
Now I've smoked my backey,
Let's have a bit of crackey
Till the boat comes in.

Dance to thy daddy, sing to thy mammy,
Dance to thy daddy, to thy mammy sing;
Thou shalt have a fishy on a little dishy,
Thou shalt have a fishy when the boat comes in.

Bobby Shaftoe
Bobby Shaftoe's gone to sea,
With silver buckles at his knee;
He'll come home and marry me,
Bonny Bobby Shaftoe.

Bobby Shaftoe's bright and fair,
Combing down his yellow hair;
He's ma ain for ever mair,
Bonny Bobby Shaftoe.

(John Bell's *Rhymes of Northern Bards*, 1812)

Bobby was thought to be one of the Shaftoes of Benwell. He was the last male heir, and he died when he was only twenty-one. The Benwell estate was inherited by Miss Shaftoe, who split it up and sold it off in lots. (*Allan's Tyneside Songs*)

Pease Pudding

Pease pudding hot,
Pease pudding cold,
Pease pudding in the pot
Nine days old.

Pease pudding is made by first soaking and then simmering
dried split peas until soft and thick and then adding a beaten
egg and seasoning. These days it is usually pressed into a
baking dish and finished off in the oven.

*Inside Harold Hill and Son Ltd. Newcastle upon Tyne,
early 1960s*

The man wi' the broon topcoat

"If thor's a man wiv a broon topcoat on calls, say aw's not in, Joe!" Them wes the vary words me maistor said te me one mornin.

Me maistor wes one o' them sort o' cheps that cud spend money a lang way faster then he cud myek't. In fact, he wes one o' them cheps that wad tyek all, an' nivvor dream o' payin' owt, so aw wassent astonish'd when he tell'd us te say he wassent in if a chep call'd wiv a broon topcoat on. So aw sets me-sel' agyen the window, as aw might see onybody that com doon the yard. Aw wad be there aboot half-an-oor when aw sees a fellow, wiv a broon topcoat on, myek tewards the shop.

"Here he is, maistor!" aw says. Thor wes ne chance o' getting away, so me maistor scrammils intiv a big cuppord. But cuppords wes nivvor myed te haud men, or they wad had ne shelves in. So the gov'nor had te dubbil hi'sel' up at the bottom, i' the kumpney ov a poke o' coals. So aw locks the door, an' puts the key i' me pocket.

"Is yor maistor in?" says the man wi' the broon topcoat, as he open'd the door an' teuk a seat.
"No!" aw says.
"Hoo lang will he be?" says he, as he drew a fob oot of his pocket, an' started te fill his pipe.
"Aw cannet say, a noor or two!" says aw, an' aw thowt that wad frighten him. But no, there he sat, puffin' away.
"Aw'm i' ne hurry, so aw think aw'll wait!" says he.

Thor wes a crash i' the cupperd an' the man an' me luckt roond at the door, as if we expected it wad open.

"What's that?" he says, kind astonish'd.

"Rats!" aw says; "wor awfully troubled wi rats here!"

"Thor big uns, te myek a noise like that!" he said, an' there he sat for a full oor. But ivry noo an'then thor wes a stir i' the cupboard!

"Aw've cum this mornin'," says he, te pay yor maister sum money that aw've been awn him this three months. Aw wad come afore if aw haddent been se bizzy."

Just imagine me feelings when he said this. Here wes a man cum te pay muney, i'steed o' cravin' for ony, an' the broon topcoat wes a' the cawse o' the fix we war in.

"Ye can tell yor maister aw call'd but it's hard to tell when aw'll be in the toon agyen! Gud-day!" says he.

"Let's oot, Joe!" groans a voice i' the cupperd. At last the pris'nor wes free, wiv a fyece ye wad swore had been up the chimley!

Oot the back door like a shot, an' inte the street, afore aw cud say nowt, an' aw sees me maister shake hands wiv the man in the broon topcoat an' tyek him intiv a public hoose.

Aboot an noor efter that *anuther* chep calls wiv a broon topcoat on - but it wes ne gud, me maister wes oot this time for fairs!

Scran and bullets

Dodgems at the Hoppings in the late 1950s

*Aa wes in the baker's shop an' aw pointed tae a grand luckin' cake an'
aa says, "Is that a cream cake or a meringue, hinney?"
"You wes reet the forst time," says she "it's a cream cake."*

Black Bullets

Jesmona Black Bullets are hard, minty-flavoured boiled
sweets that are still very popular today. There is a story that
the shape and size of these bullets is due to them being
made in musket ball moulds!

*"Hey, mister! Hoo much are thy black bullets?"
"A penny each, hinny."
"Hoo lang will ye let's hev it in ma mooth for a ha'penny?"*

The Belles of the Barbary Coast, Naughty-Ninety Girls at the Hoppings in the late 1950s

Dainty Dinah Toffees

These were another favourite, made locally at Chester-le-Street in Horner's huge factory on a five acre site that employed two thousand people. These toffees were once exported to one hundred and fifty countries, but the factory closed in the 1960s and was demolished in 1989. Gainsborough's 'Red Boy' brand of toffee was made by Cremona in Benton, Newcastle, on a site that is now a supermarket.

Cheese Savoury

This filling for stotties is made with finely chopped raw onions, grated cheese and shredded raw carrot bound together with mayonnaise or salad cream – not too much, though, because it will make your stottie soggy!

Carlings

Carlings are dried peas steeped in water and fried in butter, traditionally served on Carling Sunday, the fifth Sunday in Lent. Once when there was a famine in Newcastle a ship arrived with a cargo of dried grey peas, and it is said that this may be the source of the tradition.

The Singin' Hinny – "...the finest thing worl' hes ivver gin ye"

These are made on a griddle or a heavy flat frying pan, and they are ready when they stop singin'. The ingredients include lard, butter, currants, baking powder, salt and soured milk. These were mixed to a soft dough and cooked on a griddle, turning and flattening them as necessary until they stop singin'.

Richard Oliver Heslop was an iron merchant and also a writer of Tyneside songs, including eight verses on the singin' hinny. Here is the first one:

Sit doon, noo, man alive!
Te tell ye aa'll contrive
O' the finest thing worl' hes ivver gin ye, O.
It's not fine claes nor drink,
Nor owt 'at ye can think,
Can had a cannie up ti singin'-hinny, O
Sing hi, the Pudding' Chare an' Elwick's lonnin', O!

Panhaggerty

This is a dish of sliced potatoes, onions, butter, seasoning and grated cheese with a nicely browned top. Sometimes it also has meat added. Other dishes made in a pan include pan soddy, a type of pancake, and pan kail, a broth thickened with oatmeal.

Earl Grey and tea

Grey's Monument, 1956

Earl Grey's statue has looked down over Grainger Town since 1838, and from forty-six metres up he has a good view. Designed by Benjamin Green, it was carved by Edward Hodges Baily, who was also responsible for Nelson's Column in Trafalgar Square. Charles Grey, second Earl Grey (1764–1845) became Prime Minister in 1830, introduced the Great Reform Bill in 1832 and inherited Howick Hall, near Alnwick, from his uncle. Howick Hall remains in the same family today, with outstanding gardens which are open to the public at certain times of the year. Its Earl Grey Tearoom offers elegant surroundings for this special tea that was blended by a Chinese Mandarin to suit the water at Howick, so there is no better place to taste it.

Bergamot was used to offset the taste of lime which naturally occurs in the water in that area. However, the family did not register the trademark, and so they have never received a penny from its worldwide sales. It was Lady Grey, the Prime Minister's wife, who brought the tea with her to London and served it when she was entertaining the rich and famous. Others desired to have the Earl's favourite tea, and this is how Twinings came to market it.

The Earl's heed cums tumblin' doon

In 1941 a bolt of lightning struck the statue and the Earl's head came tumbling down, ending up in a woman's fashion shop in Grainger Street. His present head was sculpted in 1948 by Ralph Hedley.

Top scran

Tilley's was one of Newcastle's finest restaurants, fondly remembered for its starched white tablecloths, waitresses in traditional black with white aprons, silver service and string quartet. Inside it was wood panelled and had a bay window with lead glazing overlooking Blackett Street, from where you could look out at Grey's monument.

Tilleys in Blackett Street, c.1900

It was frequented by businessmen and their families, as well as actors and entertainers from the Theatre Royal. It was definitely the place to be seen. Later Tilley's moved to Northumberland Street, where the restaurant was upstairs and a doorman welcomed customers at the entrance.

"I can remember my first boyfriend taking me to Tilley's – the panelled walls, white tablecloths and silver service. I thought it was great."

"We used to be taken there by my Grandpa. The waiters wore dickie-bow ties and the waitresses had black dresses with white aprons. There was a waitress called Belle, and she always came and looked after us children."

"Do you remember the Eldon Grill and the Pineapple? For an exciting night out we'd go to Jim's Inn in Gallowgate for their Moroccan evenings, complete with belly-dancers! Above Murton's toyshop there were rooms, I think, where they held dances. In the Bigg Market was Balmbra's with entertainers, and you could get a good filling meal at lunchtime in the Cloth Market Café."

"When tight drainpipe trousers were all the rage we called them 'Turk's Heads', because they had no ball room and neither did the Royal Turk's Head Hotel! There were pubs that you couldn't get in unless you knocked on the door, and then a bouncer opened a wooden hatch to take a look at you to see if you could come in or not, as the case may be!"

Me tooth's pure knackin', man

There was a Geordie who wanted his tooth oot 'cos it wis knacking, so he asked the dentist hoo much it would be. The dentist said two and six with gas. The Geordie replies, "Far ower much, aa'll come when it's dayleet!"

The Keelmen

Keel boat laden with coal

These were fit, bonny laddies – it was the dream of many a lass to marry a keelman. Their blue bonnets and jackets and distinctive yellow waistcoats made them stand out, as did their muscular arms, honed to perfection with moving coal from the staithes on the quayside onto the keelboats, and then

Coal staithes on the Tyne

unloading the coal onto the ships for transportation to many places, including London. Newcastle kept the fires of London burning for many a year. The collier ships could not be loaded at Newcastle or Shields quaysides because the river was too shallow, so the coal had to be taken out in keelboats which were a flat, broad, blunt-nosed type of barge boat with a container for holding exactly eight chaldrons (2.65 tons). A 'keel-load' was a term for 21.2 tons of coal. The keelboats were just over twelve metres long and about six metres wide, with a single square sail, two oars and two iron-tipped poles for moving through shallow water, but no rudder. The hold for storing the coal was only two feet deep, so a box-like structure of wooden boards was built above the hold so that the coal could be piled up high. The captain, two crew members and a boy went on board with a good basket of food, because the journey from the staithes to the collier ships and back could take about twelve hours. The colliers had several coal portholes so that the keelmen from a number of keelboats could shovel their cargo of coal onto the ship at the same time. The keelboats had to queue to offload their coal, so there was no knowing when these muscular men, covered in coal-dust, would return to wor lass.

The keelmen lived outside the city walls in Sandgate, a poor and overcrowded area but a close-knit community. Houses were so close together that a dog could leap from one side of the street to the other, and from Side, you can still walk up Dog Leap Stairs today.

Weel may the keel row

As aw was gawn thro' San'get, thro' San'get, thro' San'get,
As aw was gawn thro' San'get, aw he'rd th' lasses sing:
Weel may th' keel row, th' keel row, th' keel row,
Weel may th' keel row that maw lad's in!

He wears a blue bonnet, a bunch of ribbons on it;
He wears a blue bonnet, a dimple in his chin:
An' weel may th' keel row, th' keel row, th' keel row,
An' weel may th' keel row, that maw lad's in!

(In *Allan's Tyneside Songs* it says that this version of *The Keel Row* was around before 1760.)

The days of the keelboats ended with the introduction of steam power. In the 1850s the *John Bowes*, the first steam-driven collier, pioneered the way and later the River Tyne was deepened to allow new steamers to load at the Quayside.

A Tow for Nowt

A steamboat man named Forster, belonging to the Tyne, was about to proceed up the river to Newcastle from Jarrow in his tug boat when he was accosted by an impecunious keelman who wanted a tow up to the Mushroom "for nowt."

"Mr Forster, hinny!" he shouted, "give us a tow, hinny; give us a tow up to the Mushroom, hinny!"
"How do you know my name's Forster?"
"Oh, aw knaw yor nyem's Forster, hinny. I've knawn ye awll yor life. I knew your fether afore ye. He was a canny chep, your fether. He was particular fond o' me, yor fether was. Give us a tow, hinny!"

"Well, fling us your rope," says Forster.
"There ye are , hinny. Yor the model o' yor fether, hinny; the model o' yor fether. Fling us off at the Mushroom, hinny – at the Mushroom! Aye! Yor the model o' yor fether."

So Forster made the tow rope fast, and began to steam up the river. Now Forster was rather fond of a practical joke, and he thought it would be a good one not to fling the rope off at the Mushroom, but to tow him up to the bridge, about a mile higher up. So on approaching the Mushroom, the keelman sang out, "Now, Mr Forster, hinny, fling hor off, hinny, fling hor off."
Forster took no notice.
"Fling the rope off, hinny; fling the rope off. Here's the Mushroom."
Forster steered steadily on.

"Fling the rope, Forster. Why, man, fling the rope off. Why! Ye mun be a bad 'un. Ye are a bad 'un. Ye always war a bad 'un; and yor fether was a bad 'un afore ye!"

John Atlantic Stephenson

The Quayside

The quayside was not all coal and keelboats. It was also a place of hustle and bustle with many sellers and entertainers, and always busy with the importing of butter, eggs, meat and cereals from Scandinavian countries and the exporting of coal, cement, machinery and chemicals all over the world.

There were all sorts of things sold on the Quayside, including 'yalla clay' rolled up in balls and used for smartening up doorsteps, making them a nice yellowish colour as described in the popular, old song *Cushie Butterfield* written by a pitman and music hall entertainer, George Ridley. However Cushie's family and other people mentioned in this song were very cross about what was said about them and George had to keep a low profile for a while!

Cushie Butterfield (A selection from the many verses.)

Aw's a broken-hearted keelman an' aw's owerheed in luv,
Wiv a young lass in Gyetsheed an' aw calls her me duv;
Her neyn's Cushie Butterfield an' she sells yalla clay,
An' her cusin is a muckman an' they call him Tom Gray.

A woman gutting fish and some others sorting through bundles of clothing outside the Horse Inn in Sandgate, c.1890.

Chorus
She's a big lass and a bonny one an' she likes her beer;
An' they call her Cushie Butterfield an' 'aw wish she wes here.

Ye'll oft see hor doon at Sandgate when the fresh herrin cums in;
She's like a bagful o' sawdust tied roond wiv a string;
She wears big golashes, te an' her stockings was wonce white,
An' her bedgoon is laelock, an' her hat's nivvor strite.

She says, "The chep that gets me'll heh te work ivry day,
An' when he cums hyem at neets he'll heh te gan an' seek clay;

An' when he's away seekin't aw'll myek balls an' sing,
Weel may the keel row that maw laddie's in."

Mark Toney Ice Cream Van

I remember eating Mark Toney's delicious ice cream and the flamboyant character Prince Monolulu, who was a tipster and had a pitch at the Quayside Market where my uncle traded. I always thought he was from around here and just dressed up as part of his way of attracting customers, but I found out recently that he was Danish and born in St Croix in the Virgin Islands, and he had travelled the world. His real name was Peter Carl MacKay, I think.

Baltic, a contemporary art space in what was the Baltic Flour Mill & the Millennium Bridge

Sage music centre on the Gateshead Quayside

Today the quayside still holds a popular market on Sundays, and there are upmarket places to eat and drink. Across the River Tyne the Sage Music Centre, designed by Sir Norman Foster, glistens and the old Baltic flour mill, now a contemporary art gallery, stands proud at the far end of the blinking-eye Millennium Bridge which has become as much an icon of Newcastle as the Tyne Bridge.

It's starvation on the river!

When the Tyne froze over on the 15th January 1814, a Dutch seaman went out with beef-bones attached to his shoes and a large pole in his hand to test whether the ice could take his weight. It did not take long for the ice to draw the crowds.

The Freeze up in February 1947, The 183 tram and the 34 trolley bus in front of the Central Station

Skaters arrived, fires were lit on the ice, races took place (with and without skates), groups played football and quoits, booths were set up to sell 'spirituous liquors', fruit and cake sellers did a roaring trade and the music of fiddlers and pipers added to the fun which continued into the night by the light of the moon. The ice was so solid that even a horse and sledge could cross it! The only problem was the rise and fall of the tide which loosened the ice at the edges of the river, but this was overcome by placing gangways between the river bank and the ice; the out-of-work keelmen charged a toll to cross. This Frost Fair continued until the ice finally broke up on 6th February.

'Cuckoo Jack' was skilled at recovering things lost in the river, such as boats that had sunk, watches, money and even dead bodies. He brought hundreds of corpses to the 'Deed House' which stood near the mouth of the Ouseburn. It is said he was a good-natured person and returned his finds to the owners for a 'trifling remuneration'!

Takin' coals tiv Newcastle

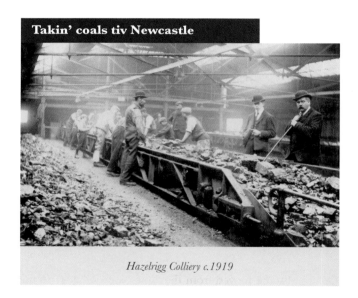

Hazelrigg Colliery c.1919

The bonny pit laddie, the canny pit laddie,
The bonny pit laddie for me, O!
He sits in his hole as black as a coal,
And brings the white siller to me, O!

Coal cart at Maria Pit, 1948

The pits in and around Newcastle were prolific in providing coal, not only for local use but for London, Indian mills, European gasworks and Spanish railways. The enormous Northumberland Dock was built in 1859 and others were to follow.

Coal had to be moved from the Newcastle collieries to the staithes on the Tyne, and traditionally this would have been by carts drawn by horses. The shortest route for a new wagon way from the Spital Tongues Colliery would have been directly to Benwell or Elswick, but Newcastle's old stone-arched bridge prevented the collier ships from reaching these places and keelboats would have to be used, adding to the expense.

To overcome these difficulties William Gilhespie, an engineer with offices in Collingwood Street, designed a two-mile-long tunnel, about twenty-six metres below ground at its deepest point, which would bring the coal to the mouth of the Ouseburn. Completed in 1842, it was named the Victoria Tunnel after the Queen, and its opening was cause for a great celebration when local VIPs and a band of musicians travelled through the tunnel in wagons. As the colliery was about sixty-eight metres higher than the Quayside, the wagons travelled down this one-in-ninety slope by gravity and were pulled back up when empty using a rope and a 40hp steam engine. Each wagon held a 'chaldron' (2.65 tons), and it was planned that a target of thirty-two wagons per train, three times an hour could be reached if necessary.

When Spital Tongues Colliery closed in 1860, the tunnel became disused and only came into use again as an air-raid shelter in the Second World War. Nowadays guided tours of the Victoria Tunnel are organised by the Ouseburn Trust.

I heard of this of this man in Gateshead who had a new grandchild and didn't seem very pleased about it. When asked why he was so upset about the new bairn he said, 'Weel, pet, it's reet bad, like. The bairn wes born in Peterlee and a divvin't want him talkin' like a pit-yakker, hinney!'

Royalty

Charles II decreed that a fixed amount of one shilling (5p) for every ton of coal exported from the Tyne to an English port must be paid to the Duke of Richmond, his illegitimate son. This payment was called a royalty.

The Blaydon Races

Balmbra's Music Hall, 1976

George Ridley, who wrote and sang *The Blaydon Races*, was born in Gateshead in 1835 and worked in the pits from eight years of age. He eventually became a wagon-rider, but while riding his train of wagons down an incline he had an accident and was badly crushed. This ended his ability to work and he began writing and singing comic songs in the music halls. Copies of his songs were sold, and he published *George Ridley's New Local Song Book, Price One Penny*. Unfortunately, he never fully recovered from his terrible accident and he died in 1864.

Aw went to Blaydon Races, 'twas on the ninth of Joon,
Eiteen hundred an' sixty-two, on a summer's efternoon;
Aw tyuk the bus frae Balmbra's, an' she wis heavy laden,
Away we went alang Collingwood Street, that's on the road to Blaydon.

O lads, ye shud only see us gannin',
We pass'd the foaks upon the road just as they wor stannin';
Thor wes lots o' lads and lassies there, all wi' smiling faces,
Gawn alang the Scotwood Road, to see the Blaydon Races.

We flew past Airmstrang's factory, and up to the "Robin
Adair",
Just gannin doon te the railway bridge, the bus wheel flew off
there.
The lasses lost their crinolines off, an' the veils that hide their
faces,
An' aw got two black eyes and a broken nose in gan te
Blaydon Races.

Chorus: O lads…

When we gat the wheel put on away we went agyen,
But them that had their noses broke, they cam back ower
hyem;
Sum went to the dispensary, an' uthers to Doctor Gibbs,
An' sum sought out the Infirmary to mend their broken ribs.

Chorus: O lads…

Noo when we gat to Paradise thor wes bonny gam begun;
Thor wes fower-and-twenty on the bus, man, hoo they
danced an' sung;
They called on me to sing a sang, aw sung them "Paddy
Fagan",
Aw danced a jig an' swung my twig that day aw went to
Blaydon.

Chorus: O lads...

We flew across the Chain Bridge reet into Blaydon toon,
The bellman he was callin' there – they call his Jacky Brown;
Aw saw him talkin' to sum cheps, an' them he was persuadin'
To gan an' see Geordy Ridley's concert in the Mechanics Hall
at Blaydon.

Chorus: O lads...

The rain it poo'd aw the day, an' myed the groons quite
muddy,
Coffee Johnny had a white hat on – they war shootin' 'whe
stole the cuddy'.
There wes spice stalls an' monkey shows, an' aud wives selling
ciders,
An' a chep wiv a happeny round aboot shootin' "Now, me
boys, for riders."

The Blaydon Races were horse races held in Blaydon on the
Gateshead side of the river. Balmbra's was in the Bigg
Market, and was the starting point for the horse-drawn bus
which travelled along Collingwood Street and the Scotswood
Road past Armstrong's Factory, now BAE Systems and under
threat of closure.

The Blaydon Races is now a road race of 5.9 miles attracting
over four hundred runners, starting at Balmbra's in the Bigg
Market, with the route going along Collingwood Street and
Scotswood Road to the George Ridley pub in Blaydon.

Broons aal roond

" Aa'll hev a bootle o' dog."

"Why di ye call it that for, like?"

"'Cos it bites yer legs, man."

'Jorney inta Space' and 'Milk of Amnesia' were other local names for Newcastle Broon.

The distinctive smell of Newcastle Broon Ale being brewed used to waft over Newcastle United supporters, especially in the Gallowgate end of St James' Park. Colonel Jim Porter launched this beer in 1927, and it is said the police asked him to make it less strong as their cells were full of drunks! In the 1960s the Newcastle Brewery, with its blue star logo, merged with Scottish Brewers to form Scottish and Newcastle Breweries Ltd. They sponsored Newcastle United's football strip from 1995 until 2000, and Broon Ale continued to be made from this site where thousands of people were employed until it closed in 2005. In 2007 the demolition of the brewery began, and in 2008 Sir Bobby Robson set away the charge to blow up the old Barrack Road bottling plant – the end of an era as well as the smell! Sir Bobby was manager of Newcastle United from 1999 until 2004, and there is a sculpture of him by Tom Maley outside St James' Park. An East Coast locomotive is also named after him, and the Sir Bobby Robson Cancer Trials Research Centre at the Freeman Hospital is an amazing facility for Newcastle.

Howay, the lads: Newcastle United Football Club has played at St James' Park since 1892, and their black and white kit is probably the reason they are called the Magpies. This is also the colour scheme for St James' Metro Station, which opened in 1982 with its black and white striped walls and the handprints and footprints of Newcastle United players decorating the concourse.

Newcastle United Football Team c.1910

Hoer's ma brains

A local farmer's daughter was somewhat annoyed by the attentions of her father's ploughman, and she asked her father to put a stop to his advances. The farmer found that his man was in the habit of hanging about the farmhouse at night awaiting the opportunity to speak to the young woman, and he determined to give him a fright. So he loaded an old blunderbuss with cold porridge, and the next night he awaited the appearance of the love-sick ploughman. That worthy put in his appearance at about the usual time, and on seeing him the farmer fired the blunderbuss full in his face. The ploughman fell to the ground in a terrible plight, full in the belief that his last hour had come.

The noise brought out the farmhands, who went and raised him up. "Are ye much hort, man?" was the excited question.

"Aa divvent knaa," he exclaimed, as he wiped the porridge from his beard, "but heor's ma brains aall ower ma hands an' fyece!"

Munitions and ships

Armstrong Works at Elswick, c.1900

William George Armstrong (1810–1900) set up a factory on the Quayside at Elswick to manufacture hydraulic equipment, including cranes which could unload ships faster than ever before. Armaments were also made there, and when he surrendered his patents for guns to the British government in 1859 he received a knighthood making him Lord Armstrong of Cragside. Hydraulic equipment for the Swing Bridge, which opened in 1876, was made here; Armstrong desperately needed this bridge so that he could ship out the heavy guns he supplied to foreign navies. The first ship to be launched from the Elswick yard was the Austro-Hungarian torpedo cruiser *Panther* in 1885, and in 1888 the first battleship, the *HMS Victoria*, was completed. By 1895 the Elswick factory employed 11,000 workers.

Sir Joseph Swan, scientist and partner in the Newcastle department store Mawson, Swan and Morgan, invented the filament light bulb, and in the 1880s his store and Mosely Street were lit with his incandescent lamps. He was a friend of the Armstrongs, and Cragside, the first house in the world to be powered by hydro-electricity, was fitted with Swan's new light bulbs.

After Armstrongs merged with Vickers, tanks and armaments were made at the site during the Second World War. In the 1950s Vickers-Armstrong and the surrounding industries employed 25,000 workers, and the site stretched three miles along the Tyne. BAE Systems are now the owners and they have announced that they propose to close the site at the end of 2013.

The Colley and the Knocker-upper

Swan Hunter workers coming off shift during the building of RMS Mauretania. She was launched in 1906 and held, for twenty-two years, the Blue Riband for the fastest ship crossing the Atlantic

Colley wiv a lamp, Colley wiv a leet,
Colley wiv a little dog barkin' at his feet.

The colley would come round at dusk to light the street lamps, and I remember watching out for him to light the lamp at the end of our road.

Many of the factory workers lived near the works and walked to work; some had housing provided by the factory, you know. If you had to get up early, a knocker-upper would come round and knock on the windows with a long stick. They'd keep on and on until they knew you were out your bed.

You know, pit workers, they were also wakened by a knocker who hammered and hammered on the door with a wooden mell. They'd chalk the time they wanted up on their door or on a bit of old slate. He was very persistent, the knocker, and would keep braying on the door 'til you opened it.

Geordie Stephenson

The unveiling of Stephenson's Monument, 1862

Very appropriately there has been a monument to George Stephenson (1781–1848) near Newcastle's Central Station since the 1860s, in honour of this man who built the first public railway system in the world. His efforts to get folk to believe that locomotives on iron rails were the future were described by George Ridley in his poem *The Stephenson Monument*.

The first locomotive that he myed,
The "Rocket" she was ca'd,
He said she'd run ten miles an hour,
The folks thowt he'd gyen mad.
These days there was ne iron rails,
The waggon-ways were wood,
He said sh'd run as hard agyen,
An' they said she nivvor could.

Stephenson met with great opposition in the fight to get his locomotive engine approved to run on the Darlington to Stockton railway, and he had to go to London as a witness before a Parliamentary Committee since the idea that railroads could make travel twice as fast as coaches and horses seemed ridiculous at the time. He was asked, "Suppose one of your trains was travelling at twenty-five miles an hour, and a cow were to get on the line, would it not be a most awkward circumstance?"

George replied, "Aye, it wad be an akward thing for the coo." Unfortunately his blunt speech and Newcastle dialect drew sneers from Londoners, and they began to call the seamen who delivered coal to London, Geordies.

Along with his son, Robert, he formed a company to make locomotives at Forth Street in Newcastle and became the world's first locomotive builder. Robert is famous for building the High Level Bridge in Newcastle and the Royal Border Bridge at Berwick-upon-Tweed.

Nae keeking, noo!

In 1850, Queen Victoria and Prince Albert opened Newcastle's Central Station, designed by John Dobson, and a delicious celebratory banquet followed. Afterwards, however, the Queen was presented with the bill! It is said that from then on the blinds in Queen Victoria's carriage were pulled down every time the Royal Train passed through Newcastle!

Grainger Town

Richard Grainger (1797–1861) presented Newcastle Town Council with a plan to redevelop the centre of the town with new streets, including Grey Street that would connect the town with the Quayside. His vision was to transform the rugged medieval Newcastle into a 'City of Palaces'. John Dobson, George Walker and John Wardle designed the classical elevations of Grey Street, and John and Benjamin Green were responsible for the section from Shakespeare Street to Market Street, including the Theatre Royal. This type of architecture has become known as 'Tyneside Classical'.

Granger Market

The building of the new Granger Town displaced some traders, and so Granger Market was built in 1835. Designed

Marks & Spencer Original Penny Bazaar

by John Dobson, it provides a covered shopping area of over eight thousand square metres. The market is an intriguing mix of all sorts of stalls, from greengrocers and butchers to bags and jewellery, as well as the famous **Marks and Spencer Original Penny Bazaar** which has been trading here since 1895, a year after Michael Marks and Tom Spencer struck up a partnership. There was no need to price anything as everything was a penny, and people were encouraged to pop in and browse by the bazaar's adverts for 'Free Admission'. In those days goods were usually kept behind the counter, but in the Penny Bazaars everything was set out so that you could see it.

Lang stockins

A pit-yakker entered a drapery shop in Newcastle and the master of the establishment asked him what he could serve him with. The customer asked to see some lang stockins. After seeing about a dozen pairs, he said that nyen o' them wad de for him.

"Well, how is that, my good man? These are long enough."

"That's reet, mister, but aa want a pair o' bow-legged yens!"

Shopping in the Toon – Newcastle's na aal pits and boats, pet!

Newcastle was very colourful, it was great, and I remember the match woman who sat outside Fenwick's and the flower sellers outside Binns. In the 1960s there were lots of department stores such as Mawson, Swan and Morgan, John Moses and Bainbridge's. At the corner of Grainger Street and the Bigg Market was Murton's Toyshop, and at the bottom of Percy Street on the Gallowgate corner was an antique shop with a stuffed bear outside!

Mebbies the forst department store i' the planet!

In 1849 Bainbridge's in Newcastle had twenty-three separate departments, making it one of the first department stores in the world. They had a reputation for caring for their staff and ran a hostel near the shop. The assistants and the company paid subscriptions to the Albert House Benevolent Society, founded in the 1870s, and this helped both past and present employees if they were in need, whether they had paid in or not.

Bainbridge & Co. in Market Street, c.1912

In 1953 Bainbridge's joined the John Lewis partnership, and later the store relocated to Eldon Square, keeping the Bainbridge name until 2002 when the store was re-branded as John Lewis.

Oooo laah, laah, hinney, get yirsel tiv the Toon for one iv them frocks!

Fenwick's store opened on Northumberland Street in Newcastle on 23rd March 1882, with its first sale, a sealskin handbag, being returned fifty years later so that the store could keep it as a souvenir. The first advertisement in the Newcastle press declared 'Nouveautés Exclusives' 'which cannot fail to please the refined taste…' There were no garish window displays here; the store was certainly more 'Galeries

*Fenwick Ltd. in Northumberland Street with crowds outside for
'The Great Summer Sale' 1898*

Lafayette' than 'Penny Bazaar', as indeed it still is. In 1887 Mr
Fenwick went off to the Riviera hotels to sell gowns for all
occasions to the wealthy women who were over-wintering
there. In 1890 in the adjoining premises Fenwick opened the
Eastern Art Store, which sold Liberty fabrics and had a public
tearoom, the first in a business house in Newcastle. The next
year their shop in New Bond Street, London was opened.

To show off the beautiful gowns ladies were engaged to
model them in the stores, and it is said that some of them hid
miniature gin flasks in their stocking tops! Wedding dresses
were individually designed, and the seamstress would stitch a
hair from their head into the hem of every bespoke wedding
dress, for luck.

Eventually the success of the store called for bigger premises and Fenwick bought the whole block behind it, right back to Eldon Square. Knowles, the architect, re-modelled it in the style of the Le Bon Marché in Paris. One of the new departments was 'ready-to-wear' fashions. Unlike many department stores at the time the employees did not live on the premises, although they were provided with dinner and tea.

After the First World War, enterprising as always, Fenwick persuaded a local munitions factory to make toys and novelties for their Christmas shoppers. Over the years more property has been bought up and the store has been through several redesigns to keep up with the times. In the 1960s a state-of-the-art air-curtain entrance was installed, and this modern, glittering, department store employed over 1,200 staff.

Their first animated Christmas window display, in 1971, drew the crowds and they still do, with customers returning year after year over the festive period to enjoy the magic of this Christmas extravaganza. Newcastle is Fenwick's head office, their flagship store and one of the largest department stores in Britain. The company now has eleven stores in different parts of the country, including London, York, Leicester and Colchester – but it all started in Northumberland Street!

The thrupenny loaf

A little chimney sweep once entered a shop near the pit and asked for a thrupenny loaf of bread. The shopkeeper handed

Horse-bus near the High Level Bridge, 1931

him one. The boy looked at it, and said it was a "smaal yen". "Oh!" said the shopman, "it will be less to carry."

The lad put tuppence-ha'penny on the counter, and then he left. The shopkeeper hastened to the door and shouted for him to come back, as he had not left money enough. "Oh!" said the lad, "it'll be less to coont!"

Haaks's men at the Battle of Waterloo

This is a famous story by John Atlantic Stephenson (his middle name refers to where he was born in 1829), telling

Ned White's tale of how Haaks's men allegedly won the Battle of Waterloo! Hawks and Company had an iron foundry works in Gateshead, and fulfilled government contracts for the supply of armaments during the Napoleonic War. Some of their workers joined the armed Forces to fight against the French.

Man, aa fell in wi' Ned White the other day. Ye knaa Ned and the other twenty-fower o' Haaks's cheps went out te the Peninsular Wa, where Wellin'ton was, ye knaa. See, as we wor hevin' a gill tegithor, aa says te him, "Ned, d'ye mind when ye wor in the Peninsular War?"

"Aa should think aa de,"says he.

"Did ye ever fall in wi' Wellin'ton?" says aa.

"Wellin'ton!" says he. "Wey, man, aa knaa'd him. Wey, just the day afore the Battle o' Waterloo he sent for me. 'Ned,' he says, 'tyek yor twenty-fower cheps,' he says, 'an gan up and shift them Frenchmen off the top o' yon hill.'

"'Als reet, says aa, 'but it winnit tyek all the twenty-fower,' aa says.

"'Ah, but it's Napoleon's crack regiment,' he says, 'ye'd bettor teyk plenty.'

"'Aal reet,' aa says, 'we'll suen shift them.'

"So doon aa cums te the lads an' aa says, 'Noo, ma lads, Wellin'ton wants us te shift yon Frenchmen off the top of yon hill. Heor, Bob Scott, come here, hoo mony Frenchmen are there up yonder?'

"'Aboot fower hundred,' he says.

"'Hoo mony on us will it tyek te shift them, Bob?'

"'Oh, ten,' says Bob.

"'Wey, we'll tyek fourteen,' aa says, 'just te humour the aad chap.'

"'Aal reet,' they says. So off we set at the double alang the lonnen, but just as we turned the corner at the foot of the hill, whee should we meet but Bonnipart hees-sel on a lily-white horse, wiv a cocked hat on. 'Where are ye off te, Ned?' says he.

"'Wey, te shift yon Frenchmen off yon hill!'

"'Whaat!' he says. 'Wey, that's me crack regiment,' he says.

"'Nivvor mind that,' aa says, 'Wellin'ton says we hev te shift them, and shifted they'll be noo!'

"'Get away, man, ye're coddin',' says he.

"'Ne coddin' aboot it,' aa says; 'cum by!'

"'Haud on, then,' he says, and he gallops reet up the hill on his lily-white horse and shoots oot, 'Gan back, ma lads, gan back! Heor's Ned White frae Haaks's and fourteen of his cheps comin' up te shift ye. Ye hevvent a happorth of chance!' Did aa ivvor see Wellin'ton? Wey, man, ye should think shyem!"

Ah canna believe that, hinny!

In the British Library is a recording of Sparkie the budgie from Newcastle singing:

"Wor little spuggy ran oop the wahter spoot.
The rain came doon and washed oor spuggy oot."

It is said that Sparkie could say five hundred words and recite eight nursery rhymes, and he made a record to help owners to teach their birds to talk. Clever Sparkie won a talking

Dining Room, Kenton in the 1950s

competition run by the BBC in 1958, and featured in commercials for Capern's bird seed. When he died in 1962 his body was stuffed and given to a Newcastle Museum!

Div ye knaa that aal these cum frae Newcassel, like?

The Turbinia , built by Parsons and Hood in 1894, was the first ship to be propelled by turbines and could travel at 30 knots. In 1897, she was the fastest ship in the world and is now proudly displayed in Newcastle's Discovery Museum.

Andrews Liver Salts: Mr Scott, a lay preacher at St Andrew's Church in Newcastle, invented a remedy for indigestion in 1903 and named it after his church.

Delrosa Rose Hip Syrup: Mr Scott and Mr Turner invented this mixture to provide vitamin C for children whose diets were deficient. During the Second World War, local childen were paid to collect rose hips. Delrosa collected the hips from the school and the syrup was made at their factory in Wallsend.

Milk of Magnesia: First made in Newcastle by Mr Turner and Mr Phillips.

Fairy Soap: Manufactured by Hedley and Sons in Newcastle.

Lucozade: In the 1880s W. Owen opened a pharmacy in Barras Bridge. Behind the shop was a mineral water works known as the 'Lemonade Factory'. Ginger ale, lemon squash and sparkling tonic water were all made there. In the 1920s Frederick Charles Pybus, a young surgeon in Newcastle, made a sparkling energy drink from glucose and flavoured it with citrus for his many patients from Jesmond and Gosforth who were recovering from operations. His patients liked this concoction and wished to buy some when they left hospital, so they went along to Owen's pharmacy whereupon he made up the prescription and called it Lucozade.

Acknowledgements

I would like to thank the staff at Berwick-upon-Tweed library, Sarah and Pam at Newcastle City Library and everyone who shared their memories of Newcastle upon Tyne with me, especially Hugh and Diane Graham, Brian Johnson, Val Telfer and Shirley from Barter Books. A special thanks to Newcastle Libraries for their permission to use photographs from their archives and to the Mark Toney family for permission to use their photograph.